CANNABIS COOKBOOK WITH EASY MEDICAL MARIJUANA RECIPES FOR EDIBLES

Grant Horton

CANNABIS COOKBOOK WITH EASY MEDICAL MARIJUANA RECIPES FOR EDIBLES

TABLE OF CONTENTS

INTRODUCTION

As the legalization of marijuana continues to spread, our relationship with the plant flourishes and evolves. While we once kept it in air tight, hidden from sight containers, now our weed might sit on the kitchen counter next to other baking and cooking accouterments.

Cooking with cannabis is an amazing way to bring creativity and flavour together with the buzz of our much-beloved herb. So here are easy recipes to get you going in the kitchen.

Consuming cannabis in scrumptious homemade edibles is a healthier alternative to smoking, and it also offers a whole new culinary experience. Even more, eating cannabis edibles offers a much potent (and usually longer) experience than smoking.

Cooking with cannabis is a delight, and a great way to get inspired in the kitchen while still reaping the great high of your weed. The thing is, it can be quite hard to know where to get started, especially if you have never really tried cooking for yourself before. But all is not lost! In this book we have put together a list of our top easy to follow cannabis recipes that will get you started on your kitchen conᐤuests, so check 'um out!

MARIJUANA HEATH BAR COOKIES

Ingredients:

2 1/2 cups all-purpose flour 1 teaspoon salt

1 teaspoon baking soda

1 cup (2 sticks) weed butter, softened 1 1/2 cups sugar

2 eggs

1 teaspoon vanilla

1 1/2 cups chopped Heath Bar pieces (Eight 1.4 ounce bars) 1/2 cup chopped walnuts

Directions:

1. Sift together the flour, salt, and baking soda. Set aside. In a separate bowl, combine Heath Bar pieces and chopped walnuts. Set aside.

2. Beat together the weed butter and sugar. Beat in eggs one at a time, and vanilla.

3. Alternatively mix in the Heath Bar mixture and the flour mixture, a third at a time, until well blended. Chill cookie dough for at least 30 minutes (better an hour or longer).

4. Preheat oven to 350°F. On cookie sheets lined with parchment paper or Silpat, spoon out the cookie dough in small 1-inch diameter balls (size of a large marble). Place dough balls 3 inches away from each other on the cookie sheets. (Make sure there is plenty of room between the cookie balls, and that the cookie balls aren't too big. These cookies spread!)

MARIJUANA MAPLE SNICKERDOODLES

Ingredients:

2 cups all-purpose flour

1 1/2 teaspoons baking powder 1/4 teaspoon baking soda

1 1/2 teaspoons ground cinnamon 1/2 cup weed butter, softened

1 cup white sugar

3 tablespoons real maple syrup 1 egg

1/2 cup white sugar 1/4 cup maple sugar

Directions:

Preheat oven to 350 degrees F (175 degrees C). Stir together the flour, baking powder, baking soda, and cinnamon. Set aside.

In a large bowl, cream together the margarine and 1 cup of white sugar until light and fluffy. Beat in the egg and maple syrup. Gradually blend in the dry ingredients until just mixed. In a small dish, mix together the remaining 1/2 cup white sugar and the maple sugar. Roll dough into 1 inch balls, and roll the balls in the sugar mixture. Place cookies 2 inches apart on ungreased cookie sheets.

Bake 8 to 10 minutes in the preheated oven. Cookies will be crackly on top and look wet in the middle. Remove from cookie sheets to cool on wire racks.

MARIJUANA MALTED MILK BALL COOKIES

Ingredients:

2 1/4 cups all purpose flour 1 tsp baking soda

1/2 tsp baking powder 1/2 tsp salt

3/4 cup weed butter, room temperature 1 cup sugar

1/2 cup milk

1 tsp vanilla extract

1 1/2 cups roughly chopped maltesers/whoppers/malted milk balls

Directions:

Preheat the oven to 350F and line a baking sheet with parchment paper.

In a medium bowl, whisk together flour, baking powder, baking soda and salt.

In a large bowl, cream together weed butter and sugar until light and fluffy. Stir in milk and vanilla, then gradually blend in the flour mixture. Do not overmix; stir only until no streaks of flour remain. Stir in the chopped Maltesers/Whoppers/Malted Milk Balls.

Drop into 1-inch balls (tbsp sized balls) on the prepared baking sheet and bake for 12-14 minutes, until lighty browned.

Cool on baking sheet for 2-3 minutes, then transfer to a wire rack to cool completely.

MARIJUANA CARAMEL WALNUT DREAM BARS

Ingredients:

1 box yellow cake mix

3 tablespoons weed butter softened 1 egg

14 ounces sweetened condensed milk 1 egg

1 teaspoon pure vanilla extract 1/2 cup walnuts finely ground 1/2 cup finely ground toffee bits

Directions:

Preheat oven to 350. Prepare rectangular cake pan with cooking spray then set aside. Combine cake mix, weed butter and one egg in a mixing bowl then mix until crumbly. Press mixture onto bottom of prepared pan then set aside. In another mixing bowl combine milk, remaining egg, extract, walnuts and toffee bits. Mix well and pour over base in pan. Bake for 35 minutes.

MARIJUANA WHITE CHOCOLATE, CRANBERRY AND MACADAMIA NUT COOKIES

Ingriedients

3 cups all purpose flour 1 teaspoon baking soda 3/4 teaspoon salt

1 cup (2 sticks) weed butter, room temperature 1 cup (packed) golden brown sugar

3/4 cup sugar 2 large eggs

1 tablespoon vanilla extract

1 1/2 cups dried cranberries (about 6 ounces)

1 1/2 cups white chocolate chips (about 8 1/2 ounces)

1 cup coarsely chopped roasted salted macadamia nuts (about 4 1/2 ounces)

Directions:

Preheat oven to 350°F. Line 2 large rimmed baking sheets with parchment paper. Sift first 3 ingredients into medium bowl. Using electric mixer, beat butter in large bowl until fluffy. Add both sugars and beat until blended. Beat in eggs, 1 at a time, then vanilla. Add dry ingredients and beat just until blended. Using spatula, stir in cranberries, white chocolate chips, and nuts.

For large cookies, drop dough by heaping tablespoonfuls onto prepared sheets, spacing 21/2 inches apart. For small cookies, drop dough by level tablespoonfuls onto sheets, spacing 11/2 inches apart.

Bake cookies until just golden, about 18 minutes for large cookies and about 15 minutes for small cookies. Cool on sheets. Do ahead Can be made ahead. Store airtight at room temperature up to 2 days or freeze up to 2 weeks.

MARIJUANA ORANGE DARK CHOCOLATE CHIP COOKIES

Ingredients:

1/2 c weed butter

1/2 c butter flavor shortening 3/4 c white sugar

3/4 c light brown sugar 2 eggs

2 tsp mexican vanilla

grated rind from one orange juice from one orange

2 1/4 c all purpose flour 1 tsp baking soda

1 tsp salt

2 cups Hershey's Special Dark chocolate chips

Directions:

Preheat oven to 350.

Silpat cookie sheets, use parchment, or grease lightly.

Cream the weed butter, shortening, brown sugar, white sugar, orange juice, and vanilla until light and fluffy. Add eggs one at a time beating well after each addition.Combine the dry ingredients and the orange peel and stir in to the creamed mixture. fold in chocolate chips lightly and chill for 20 minutes or so.

Drop by rounded teaspoonfuls on baking sheet and bake 8-10 minutes until light golden brown and still soft, but set in the middle. Let cool on the cookie sheet for 5 minutes and then remove to cooling rack or counter. 3-4 dozen cookies.

MARIJUANA PUMPKIN MUFFINS

Ingriedients:

1/2 cup canned pumpkin puree

1 egg

3/4 cup milk

2 Tbsp. canola oil

2 cups cake flour

3 tsp. baking powder

1 tsp. ground ginger

1+1/2 tsp. cinnamon

1/2 tsp. ground cloves

1/4 tsp. salt

1/2 cup dark brown sugar, packed

1 cup fresh cranberries, finely chopped

1/4 cup granulated sugar

Weed Butter

Directions:

Combine pumpkin, egg, milk, and oil in small bowl. Sift together flour, baking powder, ginger, cloves, and salt in a large mixing bowl. Stir in brown sugar, mix well. Make a "well" in center of the flour mixture. Pour pumpkin mixture into the "well," then sprinkle with cranberries. Stir just until all ingredients are moistened; DO NOT OVER-MIX or the muffins will be tough. Spoon into 12 muffin cups. Bake at 400 degrees for 12 to 15 minutes, until a toothpick inserted in center of a muffin comes out clean. Let sit in pan 1 minute, then roll in granulated sugar while still warm. Enjoy while warm and add weed butter as desired.

MARIJUANA APPLE CORNBREAD

Ingredients

2 apples, peeled and chopped thinly 1+1/2 Cup unbleached white flour

1+1/2 cup blue corn meal (or regular yellow corn meal) 3+1/2 tsp baking soda

1/2 tsp salt

1 tbsp Sucanat (Described as unrefined natural sugar made from evaporated sugar cane juice --Ed.)

-brown sugar will work fine, though 2+1/4 cup vanilla marijuana milk

1 tsp cinnamon

1/4 cup apple sauce 2 tbsp maple syrup

Directions:

1. Preheat oven to 400°F.

2. In a large bowl, combine all ingredients except the apple.

3. Mix in the apple. Do not overmix as the bread could become tough.

4. Bake 35-45 minutes on the top shelf of the oven.

5. Bread is done when an inserted knife comes out clean, about 40 minutes.

MARIJUANA CHOCOLATE CHIP COOKIES

For decades, stoners have been eating pot cookies, and it's clear why. Cannabis cookies are ex□uisitely good to eat, can be one of the more potent edibles available, are priced fairly (usually between $5 and $20 at most dispensaries, depending on dosage) and have long-lasting effects. These decadant ladies will produce an incredibly intense body high, with moderate to high drowsiness. Pot brownies are generally not recommended for daytime use although, depending on the dose, it is possible to function while medicated

Recipe:

Chocolate chips (one 12 ounce bag) Brown Sugar (1/2 cup)

Egg (1 medium size) Granulated sugar (1/4 cup) Baking soda (1/2 tsp) Flour (1 1/3 cup)

Salt (1/2 tsp)

Cannabis butter (1/2 cup)

Note: Dosage depends on the potency of your cannabis butter.

Preheat your oven to 375 F. Next, mix both of the sugars, butter and egg in a large bowl. Do this by hand. Next, after this is mixed up, add in the baking soda and salt. Then, slowly add in the flour a little bit at a time, mixing it in after each addition. Now, add in the chocolate chips, stirring constantly. Once this mixture is thoroughly blended together, you will need to grease a cookie sheet. Use your clean hands to roll around 1 inch balls of cookie dough and place on the cookie sheet roughly 2 inches apart from each other. Place the cookie sheet in the oven and bake for 10 to 12 minutes, let cool and enjoy your medication.

MARIJUANA TRUFFLES

One of the more common marijuana edibles found at dispensaries, truffles are an extremely tasty way to medicate for many patients. However, these decadent babies are not exclusive to dispensaries. You can make your own right in your kitchen.

Ingredients:

12 oz. semi-sweet chocolate morsels

1/4 cup super fine granulated sugar

2 beaten egg yolks

1 cup finely chopped walnuts, hazelnuts or almonds

1/3 cup liqueur (Kahlua)

4 tbsp CannaButter

Directions:

Slowly melt the chocolate morsels in a fondue pot or double boiler, while steadily adding in the CannaButter. Once the butter has melted in, stirring constantly, add in the sugar until it dissolves in the chocolate and butter. Next, remove the pot from the heat source and add 2 or 3 tablespoons to the beaten egg yolks to warm them up. Once you do this, add the egg yolks with the chocolate into the pot, mixing it in thoroughly. Mix in the almonds and li□ueur and pour onto a glass brownie pan. Place in the refrigerator to solidify. After 3 or 4 hours the truffles should be hardened and you may cut and form them to your desire. Store in the refrigerator or freezer. Serve and enjoy.

MARIJUANA BANANA BREAD

Marijuana-infused banana bread is loved by Cannabis patients all over. It is a delicious way to medicate and is not overly rich and sweet like many edibles can be. The best way to make banana bread is to use medicated butter or margarine, however it can also be made using extremely finely ground Cannabis.

Materials

Baking grease

1 glass loaf-baking pan

1 stirring spoon

Ingredients

2 cups flour

3 bananas

1/2 cup sour cream or heavy whipping cream 1 cup cane sugar

2 medium-sized eggs 1 tsp baking soda

1/2 cup chopped walnuts 1/2 tsp vanilla extract

1/2 cup CannaButter (potency of bread depends on the potency of the butter)

Directions

Preheat the oven to 350 (this is important as anything over 385 degrees will kill off the THC). Beat the softened butter, eggs, sugar and sour cream (or whipping cream) in a large mixing bowl. Mix in both the vanilla as well as the baking soda. Next, slowly but steadily, add in the flour, mixing it in after each addition to the bowl. When you have mixed in all the flour, add the walnuts. Now, you add the bananas and beat them in until they are as mashed and have as little lumps as possible. Grease your pan and pour the mixture in it.

Place in the oven and bake for 55 to 60 minutes.

MARIJUANA RICE CRISPY TREATS

Making special rice crispy treats is a fun, easy and fast way to make your own marijuana edibles. The recipe calls for Cannabis-infused margarine rather than butter. To make this, simply substitute margarine for butter using the CannaButter recipe. Share these tasty treats with your friends, or hoard them all for yourself, it's up to you.

Ingredients:

1 10 oz. bag of marshmallows

6 cups Rice Krispies cereal (or similar "knock-off" brands) 1 12 oz. bag of butterscotch pieces

3 tbsp Cannabis-infused margarine

Directions:

On an extremely low heat, melt your marijuana margarine in a large saucepan or pot. You will want to make sure that it is on very low heat so that you do not kill off the THC with too high of heat. Add the bag of marshmallows and mix it until the margarine and marshmallows are thoroughly blended. Once they are blended together well, remove from the heat. Quickly, while the mixture is still hot, add the cereal and stir until it is evenly dispersed throughout the mix. Now, mix in the butterscotch pieces, stirring thoroughly.

Press your mixture into a greased baking pan and let chill for at least 45 minutes. After this time, you may cut the solidified mixture into whatever size pieces you please. Enjoy these tasty medicated snacks for a long-lasting, enjoyable effect.

MARIJUANA CHEESECAKE

Cannabis-infused cheesecake is one of the tastiest sweet edibles available. The best way to make medicated cheesecake is to use hash oil or honey oil and melt it slowly into the butter that is called for in the recipe. However, it can also be made using the traditional CannaButter recipe.

Ingredients:

1 ¾ cups finely crushed graham crackers

¼ cup finely chopped walnuts or pecans

½ tsp cinnamon

½ cup melted butter

4 - 6 grams hash oil or honey oil (BHO)

Filling

3 8 oz. bags of softened cream cheese 1 cup fine granulated sugar

2 tbsp flour

1 tsp vanilla extract

½ tsp finely shredded lemon peel 2 medium-sized eggs

1 egg yolk

¼ cup milk

Directions

Slowly melt honey oil or hash oil into the ½ cup of butter just as you would when making regular CannaButter. Next, add the cinnamon, nuts and graham crackers together in a large mixing bowl. Now, mix in the BHO butter. Once this is thoroughly mixed, press it into a non-greased 8-inch spring form pan and set it aside for the time being.

Filling

Preheat oven to 375 degrees. Whip the cream cheese, flour, sugar, vanilla and lemon peel in a mixing bowl with an electric mixer. For the next step, ensure that the mixer is on the lowest or second lowest setting. Add in the 2 eggs and the egg yolk together and wait while it is steadily mixed in. Now, slowly mix in the milk. Pour this mixture into the crust and place in a shallow baking pan. Once the oven is preheated, put the pan in the oven.

Bake at 375 for 45 to 50 minutes. When it is properly done, the middle should not really move when lightly shaken. Let cool on a wire rack for 15 to 20 minutes, loosening the sides of the spring form pan after this time. Let it cool for an additional 30 minutes. After this, completely remove the sides of the pan and let cool for another hour. Lastly, cover and let chill in the freezer for 4 hours. Serve and enjoy around a dozen servings.

MARIJUANA CHOCOLATE SPACE CAKE

Ingredients:

0.44 pounds (200 grams) white baking flour 200 centiliters milk

2 medium eggs

0.22 pounds (100 grams) powdered cacao or chocolate syrup (as much as you like)

0.40 pounds (180 grams) medicated butter (unsalted)

0.40 pounds (180 grams) powdered sugar Cake pan

Directions:

Preheat oven to 380 degrees. Put medicated butter in microwave on medium or low setting (too high of heat will eliminate the THC) until it is melted into a liquid paste. Rub non-medicated butter or Crisco on cake pan so it doesn't stick. Mix medicated butter, flour, sugar, eggs, milk and cacao (powdered chocolate or as much chocolate syrup as you like) in a large mixing bowl until the texture is smooth and lump-free. If the consistency is too li□uidy, add a little more flour and if it is too thick, add a little more milk. Pour the mixture into the "greased" cake pan. Place in the preheated oven for 21 - 23 minutes.

Take out of the oven and let stand for a half-hour. Add your favorite frosting or for an added dose, buy or make medicated frosting using buttermilk, powdered sugar and medicated butter. Frost, serve and enjoy.

MARIJUANA SCONES

Ingredients:

1 1/2 tbsp. VERY POTENT marijuana-infused butter 2 1/2 cups self-raising flour

1 pinch of salt

1 tsp. baking soda

3 1/4 tbsp margarine

1 1/2 tbsp castor sugar 2/3 cup milk

1 cup dried fruit of your choice

Directions:

First of all, you will want your cannabutter to be extremely potent, since you will be using only 1 1/2 tbsp of it. Otherwise, the effect will be fairly weak. Now, mix the flour, salt, baking soda and margarine into a large mixing bowl. When this mixture looks like breadcrumbs you have it right. Next, on low heat on a stovetop, melt the cannabutter and milk together. Now, add the milk/butter mixture and sugar into the mixing bowl that has the other ingredients and steadily knead it together. Spread the dough onto a flat surface evenly, until it is about 1" thick. Next, either use a pastry cutter or a knife to cut the dough into desired shapes. Place in an oven preheated to 380 degrees fahrenheit for 25 minutes. Take out, let cool and medicate away!

MARIJUANA CARAMEL CORN

The following is a recipe for it, and all it requires is for you to have one stick (8 tbsp.) of cannabis-infused butter. It should be unsalted if you want the best flavor. Personally, I like to make it extra-potent, but for this recipe, any butter from a dispensary should be fine, since you'll be using all of it.

Ingredients/materials:

-Pan spray -1 brown paper grocery bag -1 bag popped popcorn (just under a cup of kernels if you pop them yourself) -1 medium to large mixing bowl -1 stick or 8 tbsp cannabis-infused butter (preferably unsalted) -1/4 cup light corn syrup -1 cup brown sugar -1 tsp. baking soda-1/4 tsp caramel flavoring

Directions:

First, cut the top 25% of the brown grocery bag away (assuming it's the standard size). Now, spray the inside of the bag until it's heavily coated with the pan spray, such as PAM. Next you'll take the cooked popcorn (without any unpopped kernels) and pour the popcorn in the grocery bag. Take the canna butter, brown sugar, caramel flavoring and corn syrup and place them in the bowl and put in the microwave on medium heat until thoroughly melted, while stirring every 10 or 15 seconds. Once it's thoroughly melted and resembles sauce, then take it out and stir in the baking soda while the mixture is still hot/warm. Pour the caramel mixture over all the popcorn in the bag. Now, fold the top of the bag closed and shake vigorously for 1 – 2 minutes. You can now take it out and enjoy. It will keep either in the refrigerator or an airtight container. Just a handful or two should have you buzzing nicely. Enjoy!

MARIJUANA BUTTER COOKIES

Ingredients:

1 pound cannabutter (4 sticks)

3.5 cups all-purpose flour

1 cup powdered sugar

1 tbsp. vanilla extract

Directions:

Either let the butter sit out until softened, or microwave on very low setting, until thoroughly softened, but not liquid. Then, in a large mixing bowl, add the butter, vanilla and powdered sugar and mix thoroughly together. After you've done this, mix in the flour at about 1 cup at a time, mixing it in after each one. Putting all the flour in at once will create problems and clumps when trying to get it to a smooth consistency. After all the dough is thoroughly mixed together, form the cookies into desired forms on the cookie sheet, making sure to keep them around an inch high, so they don't get too hard and crispy.

Preheat the oven to 375 and when it's ready, put the cookies in the oven for 10 to 12 minutes, or until golden brown on top. While still warm, sprinkle more powdered sugar on top. Let cool and enjoy one of the most potent cookies you've ever had.

MARIJUANA CARAMEL SQUARES

These cannabis caramel squares with sea salt and an excellently decadent treat for you to try. The best part is that they're very easy to make.

Ingredients:

1 cup cannabutter (2 sticks or 1/2 pound)

1 cup whipping cream

1 1/2 cups brown sugar

3/4 cup sugar

1/2 cup light corn syrup

1/4 cup dark corn syrup

1 tsp. sea salt

1 tsp. vanilla

Directions:

Get out a large saucepan (at least 1/2 or 3/4 gallon capacity) and butter the bottom and sides. You can use cannabutter to do this if you have extra. Now add the 1/2 pound of cannabutter and melt it on very low heat. You do not want to use medium or high heat, because you will burn the butter and thus waste precious cannabinoids. Once the butter is belted, add the brown sugar, sugar, both corn syrups and the whipping cream, adding each ingredient a little at a time and mixing in while doing so. Now that all your ingredients are in, you can briefly raise the heat to medium-high, but no more, and bring the mixture to a boil, stirring off and on while doing so. When it first starts to boil, reduce the heat to medium or just below medium and continue to cook, stirring occasionally until the mixture reaches 248 degrees Fahrenheit.

Once the mixture has reached 248 degrees, remove it from the heat and stir in the tsp. of vanilla. After this is complete, pour the mixture into a 9" baking pan that has been lined with foil and the foil has been greased with butter. Cool it gradually at room temperature, and sprinkle with sea salt once it begins cooling. Make sure it cools completely before you use to foil to lift the brick of caramel out of the pan. Once you do this, cut the pieces into desired size s☐uares - or any shape - and enjoy these potent treats. Wrap in plastic wrap or vacuum-seal and place in refrigerator for up to a week to store.

MARIJUANA POUND CAKE

Ingredients:

1/2 pound (2 sticks) cannabutter and more butter (medicated or regular) to grease the pan

3 cups sugar

1 cup milk (2% is works best)

5 eggs

1/2 cup shortening

3 cups flour

1/2 tsp. salt

1/2 tsp. baking powder

1 tsp. vanilla extract

Directions:

Before you do anything else, preheat your oven to 350 degrees Fahrenheit and have your cannabutter sitting out at room temperature to soften. Next, use either a mixer or spoon and mixing bowl to mix the butter and shortening together. After they're throughly mixed, add the sugar, slowly mixing it in as you add it. After you do that, add the eggs one after the other, mixing these in as well. Next, add in a portion of the flour and all of the salt and baking powder. Then, add a portion of the milk. Next, add the remainder of the flour, followed by the remainder of the milk. Use the mixer to completely stir all this in, or use your spoon and mixing bowl to do it thoroughly. After this is done, mix in the vanilla extract and commence to pour onto a buttered and lightly floured pound cake pan (about 10" long x 5" wide x 4" tall) and place in the oven for anywhere between 1 and 1.5 hours. When you can stick a toothpick into the center and it comes out mostly clean with no liquidy dough, it is ready. Next, just let cool and enjoy!

MARIJUANA ORANGE CAKE

Ingredients:

2/3 cup marijuana-infused olive oil

3 blood oranges (seasonal, but regular oranges will work ok.)

1 cup cane sugar

3 eggs

1/2 cup buttermilk or unflavored yogurt

1 3/4 cup regular flour

1 1/2 tsp. baking powder

1/4 tsp baking soda

1/4 tsp. table salt

Whipped cream to for serving, if desired

Directions:

First of all, preheat your oven to 350 degrees and then begin to use a grater to grate off the peel of two of the oranges. Grate the peel into a bowl containing the sugar and mix all of it together when done with the two oranges. Now, cut these two oranges in half and separate each segment and cut these segments into ☐uarters. With the remaining orange, cut it in half and juice it into a measuring cup. Add the buttermilk or yogurt to this mixture until it is 2/3 of a cup combined. Now, while mixing in the eggs and olive oil into the bowl of sugar and orange rhine, also add the buttermilk/orange juice mixture and mix this all together. Now, put the flour, baking powder, salt and baking soda into a sifter and sift into this bowl. Now, add the quarter pieces of the oranges. Then you're going to butter a pan (roughly 9" X 5") and pour the mixture into it, subse☐uently placing it in the oven for 50 to 55 minutes. After this, take out of the oven, let cool for 5 minutes, serve and enjoy.

MARIJUANA PEANUT BUTTER BARS

Ingredients:

1 cup (2 sticks) canna butter melted over low heat

2 cups confectioner's sugar

2 cups crumbled graham crackers

1.5 cups semisweet chocolate chips

1 cup peanut butter (can be chunky or smooth) 4 tbsp. additional peanut butter

Directions:

Mix the canna butter, sugar, graham crackers, and 1 cup of peanut butter in a mixing bowl until thoroughly blended. Place and press down into an ungreased 9 x 13 baking pan (or the closest size you have). Next, take a double boiler to melt the chocolate chips and 4 tbsp. of peanut butter (you can also use a metal bowl siting in simmering water or the microwave for this step). Stir every minute or two during this process, ensuring it comes out smooth and well-blended. Spread this mixture over the mixture in the baking pan, subse□uently placing your concoction in the refrigerator for 1.5 to 2 hours. Take out of the refrigerator and cut into s□uares of your preference.

MARIJUANA SCOTTISH SHORTBREAD

Ingredients:

2 cups cannabutter

4.5 cups flour

1 cup brown sugar

Directions:

If you're short on ingredients and can't make some of the more complicated recipes, this recipe for Scottish shortbread takes the cake - no pun intended - and only calls for three ingredients. First, preheat your oven to 325 degrees Fahrenheit. Soften the butter and mix thoroughly with the brown sugar. After it is mixed, add about 3/4 of your flour, a little at a time until well blended. Next, layer a flat surface like a cutting board with the remaining flour (about 3/4 of a cup) and begin to knead the dough on it. Shape the dough into 4" x 2" rectangles that are about a half-inch high. Poke around a dozen holes in the cutout with a nail or other similar object and place on an un-greased cookie sheet. Bake in the oven for 20 - 25 minutes or until just slightly golden brown. Enjoy.

MARIJUANA ICING

Ingredients:

1 3/4 cup confectioners sugar

5 tbsp. canna butter (potent)

1 tbsp. vanilla extract

1 tbsp. milk

Directions:

First, combine the sugar, canna butter, milk and vanilla until the consistency is creamy and smooth. You may need to add sugar or milk to get to desired frosting texture. Spread over your favorite sugar cookies or decorate a cake with it. Note: for cakes you should double or triple the recipe.

MARIJUANA CINNAMON ROLLS

Ingredients:

The Dough:

2 cups cannabis flour (see recipe on site) 2 tbsp. granulated sugar

4 tsp. baking powder 1 tsp. salt

3 tbsp. canna butter

3/4 cup milk (medicated for extra potency

The Filling:

4 tbsp. canna butter 1 cup brown sugar 3 tsp. cinnamon

The Glaze:

1/2 cup powdered sugar

1/4 cup milk (medicated for extra potency

Directions:

First of all, preheat your oven to 375 degrees. In a small to medium-sized mixing bowl, combine all the filling ingredients until it forms a crumbly, but well blended mixture (hint: it helps to soften the canna butter first). Next, spread half of this mixture over the bottom of a 9" x 9" pan, or closest size you have. Now, in a large mixing bowl, combine the cannabis flour, sugar, baking powder and salt and mix together thoroughly. Slowly begin to add in more softened canna butter a little at a time until well blended and subsequently mix in the milk. Spread some canna flour on a cutting board or similar surface and roll into a 1/4" thick rectangle. With the other half of your filling, spread it on top of the rolled rectangle of dough. Next, roll the rectangle up into a log and slice into 18 eual segments or 12 if you prefer bigger rolls. Bake for 25 - 30 minutes on 375 degrees Fahrenheit. While this is baking, combine the canna milk (or regular milk) and powdered sugar in a bowl and spread on top of the rolls once out of the oven. Let cool a minute or two and prepare to get really really medicated.

MARIJUANA WHIPPED CREAM

Ingredients:

1 oz. finely ground marijuana buds or sugar leaves from harvest

2 cups heavy cream

1 tbsp. confectioner's sugar

1 tsp. vanilla extract

Double boiler

Directions:

Over medium heat in the double boiler, heat up the heavy cream, subsequently adding the ground marijuana. Simmer uncovered for 1.5 hours. Next, allow the mixture to cool slightly and pour it into an airtight container, placing the container in the refrigerator for 3 - 4 hours. Take out of the refrigerator and mix in sugar and vanilla, only beating them in for around a minute. Any excess beating or mixing can result in lumpy whipped cream. Place on your favorite desert, in hot chocolate or simply eat with a spoon as it is.

MARIJUANA BREAD

Ingredients:

4 cups cannabis flour (see recipe on site)

1.5 cups canna milk (see recipe on site)

1.5 tbsp. granulated sugar

1/2 tbsp. baking powder

1/2 tbsp. baking soda

2 tsp. vinegar (white or cider tastes best)

Directions:

First, preheat the oven to 400 degrees Fahrenheit (note, may need adjusted for high altitudes). Combine the canna flour, sugar, baking powder and baking soda, mixing together thoroughly. Next, combine the vinegar and canna milk, mixing together, before adding to the dry ingredients. After mixing thoroughly, place the dough on a floured surface and knead for a couple minutes. Now, shape the dough into a rounded ball between 1.5 and 2 inches high. Place the ball in a pan and use a knife dipped in flour to cut an "X" into the top of the ball of dough. Place in the oven for 40 minutes, subse☐uently removing from the oven and, while still hot, pouring 2 tbsp. of melted butter (preferably canna butter) over the bread. Let cool and enjoy with dip, as toast or as a sandwich. For a potent treat, use as toast with canna butter on top.

MARIJUANA BANANA BLUEBERRY SMOOTHIE

Ingredients:

1 cup canna milk

2 cups fresh blueberries

1 sliced banana

1 cup strawberry yogurt

Directions:

Put all ingredients in a blender and blend until the consistency is smooth. Pour, serve and enjoy.

MARIJUANA FLAT BREAD

Ingredients:

1 1/2 tbsp cannabis-infused olive oil

1/2 cup cold water

1 1/2 cup flour

1/2 tsp salt

Optional: Choose one of the following:

cracked black pepper, shredded cheddar cheese, sea salt, parmesan cheese, sesame seeds.

Directions:

Heat your oven to 350 and place a baking stone on the lowest rack. If you have a food processor, put the salt and flour into the bowl and mix in the water and oil until the dough comes together. If you do not have a food processor, do this step by hand. Flour a clean surface in your kitchen and knead the dough for two minutes. Cover the dough and put it in the fridge for at least a few hours, ideally overnight.

Take the dough out and separate into two equal size balls. Roll them out to 1/8 of an inch thickness, keeping the round shape. Using a round pan like a pizza sheet, sprinkle a little flour or cornmeal onto the pan and put the dough on it. You can choose to add your toppings now; sprinkle a thin layer of cheese or sea salt onto the dough. Transfer the dough onto the baking stone in the oven. Bake for eight to ten minutes, or until desired crispness. If you do not have a baking stone you can use a pizza sheet, just make sure to check the bread frequently to keep from burning.

MARIJUANA TIRAMISU MILK SHAKE

Ingredients:

5 oz. canna milk

3 scoops vanilla ice cream

2 oz. espresso or very strong coffee

1 tbsp. cream cheese

Powdered chocolate

Whipped cream (medicated whipped cream works too

Directions:

First, put the 2 ounces of espresso in a blender, subsequently pouring in the 5 ounces of canna milk. Now add the cream cheese, as well as the ice cream and blend until the consistency is smooth. After it is blended, fill a tall glass about 1/3 full, then layer with some whipped cream, a dusting of chocolate, followed by more of the blended mixture, more whipped cream and a final dusting of chocolate. Enjoy and remember that this is going to medicate you fully, due to the amount of canna milk, so plan on relaxing and/or sleeping. Great treat after dinner.

MARIJUANA CHOCOLATE MILKSHAKE

Ingredients:

3 scoops chocolate ice cream (medicated for extra potency) 1/2 cup canna milk

Chocolate syrup to taste

Directions:

Put all ingredients in a blender and mix until thoroughly blended and smooth consistency. For extra chocolate flavor and presentation, line the inside of a glass with chocolate syrup, pour the milkshake in and enjoy a tasty, medicinal treat.

MARIJUANA CINNAMON COFFEE CAKE

Ingredients: Cake:

1 1/4 cups flour (cannabis flour for extra potency)

1/4 cup canna butter

1/2 cup sugar

1/4 cup sour cream

1/3 cup canna milk (or regular milk)

2 eggs beaten slightly

2 tsp baking powder

1.5 tsp. cinnamon Topping:

1/3 cup flour

1/3 cup brown sugar

1/4 cup canna butter

1 tsp. cinnamon

Directions:

First, preheat the oven to 375 degrees Fahrenheit, subse□uently combining all ingredients for the cake batter in a large mixing bowl. After thoroughly mixing, pour the batter onto an 8 or 9-inch greased/buttered baking pan. After this combine the flour and brown sugar for the topping in a bowl, mixing in the canna butter and cinnamon after. Mix until it becomes chunky and crumbly. Spread over the batter and bake for 28 to 32 minutes.

MARIJUANA RED VELVET CUPCAKES

Ingredients:

1/2 cup canna butter

1 cup buttermilk

2 eggs

2 cups flour

1 fl. oz. red food coloring

1.5 tsp. baking soda

1 tsp. vanilla extract

1 tbsp. white vinegar

1/3 cup cocoa powder

1 tsp. table salt

Directions:

First preheat your oven to 350 degrees Fahrenheit, subsequently greasing two 12-cup cupcake sheets with butter or canna butter. In a mixing bowl mix the softened butter and sugar. After the consistency is fairly fluffy, mix in the buttermilk, eggs, food coloring and vanilla extract. Then stir in the baking soda and white vinegar. In a separate bowl, combine the flour, sugar and salt and begin to mix into the batter. After it is thoroughly blended, put batter in the greased cups and bake for 20 - 25 minutes. Let cool on a rack and add frosting if desired. Enjoy!

MARIJUANA SUGAR COOKIES

Ingredients:

1 cup softened cannabis butter

2.75 cups flour

1.5 cups sugar

1 egg

1 tsp. vanilla

1 tsp. baking soda

Directions:

Preheat the oven to 375 degrees Fahrenheit. Next, in a mixing bowl mix the flour, baking powder and baking soda. In a separate but larger bowl, mix the softened butter and sugar until the consistency is smooth, subse□uently mixing in the egg and vanilla extract. After this is done, slowly mix in the flour, baking soda and baking powder, rolling the dough into small balls and place on an unbuttered baking sheet, baking for 8 to 10 minutes.

MARIJUANA OATMEAL COOKIES

Ingredients:

3/4 cup cannabis-infused olive oil

1/3 cup honey

1 3/4 cup ripe bananas, mashed up

3/4 tsp salt

4 cups uncooked regular oats

1/2 cup nuts, chopped

1/2 cup raisins (Optional: replace with chocolate chips)

Directions

Heat oven to 350 degrees Fahrenheit. In a medium bowl mix together the honey and oil until well blended. Stir in the mashed bananas and salt, mix well. Add the oats, nuts and raisins little by little, stirring in as you go. Drop by spoonfuls onto a cookie sheet and bake for 20- 25 minutes. Allow to cool for five minutes and transfer from baking sheet to cooling rack. Serve warm.

MARIJUANA CHOCOLATE PUDDING

Ingredients:

2 cups cannabis milk

1 box instant pudding mix, chocolate (14 oz) 1/2 tsp ground cinnamon

1/2 cup frozen whipped topping, thawed

Directions:

Beat the pudding mix, cannabis milk and cinnamon with a whisk for about two minutes. Stir in the thawed whipped topping until thoroughly mixed. Refrigerate for about thirty minutes, and enjoy!

MARIJUANA LEMON BREAD

Ingredients:

6 tbsp. (3/4 stick) canna butter

1.5 cups flour

1 cup cane sugar

2 large eggs

1/2 cup milk (canna milk works too)

1/2 cup cane sugar (again)

1/2 cup chopped walnuts (optional)

1 juiced lemon

1 tsp. lemon zest (finely grated lemon peel)

1 tsp. baking powder

1/2 tsp. salt (or lemon salt)

Directions:

First, preheat the oven to 350 degrees Fahrenheit. In a small bowl, mix the flour, salt (or lemon salt) and baking powder, until blended thoroughly. In a separate but larger bowl, mix the softened canna butter, eggs and cup of sugar together. Next add the milk (or canna milk) and flour, first adding milk, then flour, then milk and then flour. Blend this thoroughly as well. Now mix in the lemon zest, followed by the nuts, if you choose to add them. Pour this mixture into a buttered and floured 9 x 5 baking pan. This is essentially the same size as is used to make banana bread loaves. Place this in the preheated oven for 60 minutes. When you take it out, let it cool a few minutes in the pan. At the end of the baking time in the oven, mix the remaining 1/2 cup cane sugar and the juice of the lemon. Make sure to mix thoroughly and use this as a glaze to pour over the cooled bread, if you choose.

MARIJUANA CASHEW COOKIES

Ingredients:

Crust:

4 tbsp (1/2 stick) canna butter

1 cup flour (can use cannabis flour too, but may affect consistency)

1/3 cup packed brown sugar

1/4 tsp. salt Topping:

1/2 cup butterscotch chips

1/4 cup light corn syrup

2 tbsp. canna butter

1 cup salted cashews

Direction:

Preheat the oven to 350 degrees Fahrenheit and put sugar in a medium mixing bowl. Blend in 2 tbsp. canna butter until the consistency resembles crumbs. Next add the flour and salt, mixing thoroughly. Press into an ungreased pan and bake for 11 - 12 minutes. In a separate container, melt the butterscotch, corn syrup and 2 tbsp. Don't boil it, just simmer. Pour over the crust, subsequently adding the cashews and let cool. Enjoy.

MARIJUANA APPLE PECAN GALAXY CAKE

Ingredients:

1 cup flour

1/2 cup whole wheat flour

1/4 tsp cinnamon

1/2 tsp baking soda

1/2 tsp nutmeg

1/2 tsp salt

1 egg

1 cup granulated sugar

2/3 cup cannabis-infused olive oil

1/2 cup pecans, chopped

1 1/2 granny smith apples, peeled and grated

1 gala apple, thinly sliced

15 pecan halves For the glaze:

1/4 cup brown sugar

2 tsp cannabis infused olive oil

2 tsp water

Directions:

Heat your oven to 325 degrees Fahrenheit. Lightly coat a 9 inch spring form pan with nonstick cooking spray. In a medium bowl, combine the cinnamon, flours, baking soda, nutmeg and salt until blended. In a large bowl, whisk the egg and sugar with the 2/3 cup cannabis-infused olive oil. Stir the flour mixture into the egg mixture, and add the chopped pecans and grated apples. Scrape into the prepared pan and flatten the top with a spatula. Arrange the apples slices on top of the edge of the cake, and arrange the pecan halves in one layer in the center.

Make the glaze in a small microwavable bowl. Mix together the brown sugar and the 2 tsp olive oil and water, and microwave in thirty second intervals until the brown sugar is melted. Brush the apples and pecans with half of the glaze and save the rest.

Bake in the center of the oven until a toothpick inserted into the middle of cake comes out clean, about 45 minutes. Remove from the oven and brush the top of the warm cake with the rest of the glaze. Remove the ring by running a knife around the outside of the cake . Gently remove cake from base. Serve with a scoop of vanilla ice cream.

MARIJUANA BROWNIES

OIL Method – What You Need

1. Oil (any other than olive oil)

2. 2.5 grams of any indica or sativa marijuana (Some that i recommend are Barneys Farm G13 Haze, Green House Seeds Cheese, or LA Confidential)

3. A Grinder

4. A Filter (coffee filter, pasta strainer)

5. Brownie mix

6. A Frying pan

7. A wood spoon

For an whole batch of brownies (1 box) a half ounce of dank or an ounce of mids is what you need. Grind up the marijuana in your grinder or a coffee grinder multiple times until it literally turns into powder.

Once the marijuana turns into a powder spread it right onto a frying pan. Its a good idea to match the frying pan to the burner size for an even cook which is important when extracting the THC. Pour oil directly onto the marijuana powder on the pan according to how much the brownie recipe asks for.

Turn the burner on low (numbers 2-3) until it starts to simmer and then lower the burner to the lowest setting (labeled as low or simmer). Leave the burner on for 2-6 hours depending on how much time you have (2 hrs is average) and stir the marijuana in the oil every 30 minutes with a wooden spoon.

When the pot is done, pour the oil mixture into a filter (coffee filter works fine) to strain all the excess marijuana out. You should be left with a musky brown color oil without any grass, stems, or seeds in it. This stuff needs to be filtered out as there is no THC left because it was extracted into the oil.

Use this oil to make the brownies by following the instructions on the brownie box. If you prefer to make weed brownies using butter rather than oil, continue reading.

BUTTER Method – What You Need

1. Butter

2. 2.5 grams of any indica or sativa marijuana (Some that i recommend are Barneys Farm G13 Haze, Green House Seeds Cheese, or LA Confidential)

3. A Grinder

4. A Filter (coffee filter, pasta strainer)

5. Brownie mix

6. A small pot and a larger pot

7. A wood spoon

In order to use butter to extract the THC and bake brownies, two pots are required, one larger and one smaller. The larger one should be filled up with clean water and the same size as the burner for an even burn. Place the smaller pot inside the larger one and throw in 2-3 sticks of butter.

Turn the burner on a low setting until the water in the larger pots begins to simmer. Once this happens, use your judgment on a good setting med – low to establish a near simmer. The water in the larger pot will heat up the THC in the marijuana in the the smaller pot with out burning it which could destroy the THC, making the brownies useless.

Proceed to leave the the burner on for 2-3 hours, or longer. Once done, pour the butter through a filter removing any seeds, stems, or left over marijuana bud which is useless since the THC is now in the butter. Spread this butter throughout the bottom of a large pan and pour the brownie mixture on top. Cook in the oven (350 degrees) for 30 minutes to an hour.

Now that you know how to make marijuana brownies using the butter method, tell us how you liked this method in a comment below!

MARIJUANA CUPCAKES

Ingredients:

1 1/4 cups flour

1/2-3/4 cup sugar (depending upon sweetness desired) 1 3/4 teaspoons baking powder

1/4 teaspoon salt 1/3 cup weed butter 1 egg, beaten

3/4 cup milk

1/2 teaspoon vanilla

2/3 cup blueberries (or whatever you wish to use) 1/3 cup chopped unblanched almonds, toasted

Directions:

1. Sift dry ingredients together to mix well.

2. Cut in the butter until mixture resembles coarse crumbs.

3. Whisk egg vigorously to incorporate air and make the eggs light.

4. Stir in egg, milk and vanilla and combine thoroughly.

5. Add to dry mixture and stir together (some lumps should remain) and add the blueberries.

6. Fill well greased muffin tins with batter until two thirds full.

7. Bake in a preheated 350°F oven for 20 minutes or until done.

Note: Makes 18 large muffins.

MARIJUANA ICED COFFEE

Ingredients:

6 oz Canna Milk

2 tsp instant coffee mix 1 tsp sugar

3 tbsp warm water

Directions:

In a jar, combine the warm water, instant coffee and sugar. Cover with lid and shake until the mixture is foamy. Pour into a tall glass filled with ice, then add the Canna Milk and stir. Add more sugar or some chocolate syrup if desired.

MARIJUANA JELLO SHOTS

Ingredients:

10 oz. marijuana vodka (green dragon)

6 oz. Jello mix

16 oz. boiling water

6 oz. cold water

Directions:

Bring the larger amount of water to a rolling boil, subse☐uently adding the Jello mix to the boiling water. Turn off the heat once the Jello has dissolved. Next add the 6 oz. cold water (to cool it down for the next step) and then add the 10.oz of MJ vodka after the cold water. Pour into shot glasses or small plastic cups and refrigerate for 3 - 5 hours, depending on temperature of the refrigerator.

MARIJUANA LATTE

Ingredients:

(1 16 oz. latte)

14 oz. canna milk

2 oz. espresso (concentrated coffee)

Flavoring such as vanilla, caramel, gingerbread syrup to taste

Directions:

For this recipe, you will need an espresso machine, which can also be purchased for as little as $40 dollars. Insert the finely ground coffee grinds into the appropriate spot in the espresso machine and begin making 2 oz. of espresso. Now, begin to steam the milk, making as little bubbles as possible and creating a creamy, hot substance (bubbles are bad and means you tried to move the cup too fast). When the thermometer in the milk shows 130 degrees Fahrenheit, stop steaming. The thermometer is behind and will take a few seconds to catch up to the actual temperature. The ideal final temp for a latte is between 140 and 150 degrees Fahrenheit. By this time, you should have stopped the espresso from dripping when it reached around two oz. Now put a little of your favorite flavor syrup into the espresso shot and swirl around. Pour the espresso and flavoring in a cup or mug.

Gently pour the milk in. Enjoy and start your day off right.

MARIJUANA VODKA

Ingredients:

Vodka

2 glass jars

1/4 ounce of stems

Directions:

Place the stems into the glass jar. Pour enough of your favorite vodka over the stems to completely submerge them. Do not fill the jar up or your vodka will be weak. Place in a dark pantry or closet and let sit for one week. Strain the stems out with a cheesecloth or with a coffee filter, transferring from one jar to another. Chill in the freezer for a few hours. Break it out and enjoy your new happy hour, 4:20 pm!

MARIJUANA COFFEE

Ingredients:

As much ground coffee as you want (press pot, Turkish press, standard coffee pot) 1 - 2 grams powdered hash or kief Water

Directions:

Put coffee in filter or press. Place kief or hash on top of grounds or mix them into the grounds. Make coffee as you normally would. This is a great recipe to start off the day. Unlike most edibles and tinctures, it will not make you hopelessly tired; it acts like a strong sativa, due to the coffee. Add sugar or a little canna milk (Bhang) for added flavor and potency.

MARIJUANA SCREWDRIVER

Ingredients:

2 oz. marijuana vodka

5 oz. fresh squeezed orange juice ice

Lemon wedge

Directions:

Put ice into a cocktail shaker. Squeeze the lemon wedge over the ice and put it inside the shaker, followed by the marijuana vodka and the orange juice. Cap and shake for about ten seconds or until mixed, and pour entire contents into a tall glass. Please drink legally according to your local laws, and responsibly. Enjoy!

MARIJUANA BLOODY MARI

Ingredients:

2 oz. Marijuana Vodka 4 oz. tomato juice

1 tbsp worcestershire sauce 1 tbsp lime juice

Tobasco sauce to taste Pepper to taste

Ice

To garnish: green olives, celery stalk

Directions:

Combine ice, Marijuana Vodka, tomato juice, worcestershire sauce, Tobasco, pepper and lime juice in a cocktail shaker. Shake for about ten seconds and pour into a tall glass.

Garnish with olives and the celery stalk. Put on your sunglasses and ride the morning out! Please enjoy legally and responsibly according to your local laws!

MARIJUANA STEM TEA

Ingredients:

Potent stems

Marijuana butter/olive oil

Water

Directions:

This recipe only reuires that you save up aminimum of 3 grams of trichome-covered stems per cup of tea. For those with higher tolerances, double the amount of stems. Also, make sure to add the butter during the brewing of the tea.

MARIJUANA TEA

Ingredients:

1/2 gram (or more) of your favorite indica, sativa or any combination of both marijuana. 3 Cups of Water

2 Tablespoons of butter

Directions:

1. First you will need to get around 1/2 gram of your favorite marijuana and grind it up as fine as you can.

(Some that i recommend are Barneys Farm G13 Haze, Green House Seeds Cheese, or LA Confidential)

2. Get small pot and put 3 cups of water in.

3. Turn the stove onto the highest setting possible and bring the water to a boil.

4. Add the 2 tablespoons of butter.

5. Add the 1/2 gram of ground up marijuana.

6. While leaving the stove on the highest heat setting and having the water violently boiling, stir every few minutes making sure that any of the marijuana on the side of the put is pushed back into the water.

Note: The point of making Marijuana tea is to extract the THC from the plant. Since THC is not soluble in water alone it requires a fatty substance to cling onto under high heat.

With the combination of the high heat from the boiling water then the butter that was added to the mixture the THC can be removed from the marijuana for drinking purposes.

7. All for the marijuana, water and butter to boil on high heat for at LEAST 30 minutes. The longer you are willing to wait the more THC that will be extracted. From my experience 30-40 minutes is usually an ideal time.

Note: While the water is boiling on high heat, the water will begin to evaporate fairly quickly. Do NOT turn it on and walk away for a half an hour or the water may be gone when you return. Watch and stir every few minutes and as extra water as needed to maintain that the water level is the same as when you started.

8. After at least 30 minutes, you can run the water through a strainer into a cup large enough to hold all the liquid. Now that the THC is removed from the marijuana and now clinging to the butter you no longer need the green.

9. The marijuana tea will be VERY hot so be VERY careful and let it cool for 5 minutes.

10. Add one of your favorite tea bags to add extra flavor, or drink as is.

11. Enjoy! As with most things consumed orally it will take 45-60 minutes for the tea to take its full effect.

Note: Be prepared to get very stoned. Even with only a 1/2 gram this recipe is much stronger then it seems. Many people have felt the effects for up to 12 hours from consuming the tea!

12. After you have made and consumed the marijuana tea, leave a comment below telling us how the process went for you and how the effects were!

MARIJUANA GARLIC BASIL GRILLED SHRIMP PASTA

Ingredients:

2 pounds shelled uncooked shrimp.

10 roma tomatoes.

3 TBLS of fresh basil.

6 cloves of garlic.

1 1/4 cup of weed oil.

2 TBLS of lemon juice.

2 TBLS of fresh parsley.

2 TBLS of white wine.

1 TBLS of fresh oregeno.

1 teaspoon of salt.

1 teaspoon of pepper.

Angel hair pasta.

Directions:

For shrimp and marinade: Finely chop 3 cloves of garlic, 2 TBLS of fresh pareley and 1 TBLS of fresh oregeno and place in a bowl.

Add in 3/4 cup of olive oil, lemon juice, salt, pepper, white wine.

Mix.

Add in shrimp.

Let marinade for three hours.

Grill on low medium heat.

Sauce: chop roma tomatoes, 3 cloves garlic and basil.

Place chopped tomatoes, garlic and basil in a sauce pan.

Add 1/2 cup of weed oil.

Add salt pepper.

Cook for 5 minutes while stirring.

Combine: place sauce on cooked angel hair and then add grilled shrimp.

MARIJUANA CREAMY BASIL CHICKEN PASTA

Ingredients:

1 pound champanelle or gemelli noodles

1 pound (about 2 large) boneless, skinless chicken breasts, cubed

½ cup breadcrumbs

¼ cup weed oil

6-8 cloves garlic, minced

2 cups chicken broth

1 1/2 cups heavy cream

1 teaspoon salt

1/2 teaspoon pepper

2-3 cups finely shredded Fontina cheese

1 cup chopped fresh basil

Directions:

Boil pasta per package directions. Drain (do not rinse!) and put back into pot. Add about a tablespoon of olive oil and then cover to keep warm.

While the pasta is boiling chop chicken and place in zip top storage bag. Add breadcrumbs shake and use your hands to press crumbs into chicken until completely coated and most of the crumbs are no longer loose.

Heat weed oil over medium heat in a large frying pan. Add chicken and toss occasionally so that all sides get browned. About 7 minutes in add garlic and toss. Try to toss this

instead of 'stirring' it, this will help the breadcrumbs stay attached to the chicken. Cook for about 3 more minutes (check largest piece to make sure its done) and remove chicken from pan.

If there is a ton of oil left in the pan pour most of it out, if not, add chicken broth, cream, salt and pepper. Bring to a boil then add cheese, bring back to a boil and cook, whisking occasionally for 5 minutes. Add basil and boil, whisking occasionally, for another 5 minutes. Pour over pasta and stir until combined. Garnish with basil.

MARIJUANA BARBECUED BEEF SANDWICHES

Ingredients:

3 pounds beef chuck

2 onions, chopped

1 (28 ounce) can diced tomatoes, with juice

1/2 cup distilled white vinegar

1/2 cup water

3 tablespoons sugar

1/3 (10 fluid ounce) bottle Worcestershire sauce salt and pepper to taste

2 tablespoons of weed butter

Preparation:

1 Place roast in a Dutch oven, and sprinkle with chopped onions. Cover with tomatoes, water, sugar and Worcestershire sauce. Season with salt and pepper.

2 Cook over medium heat with lid slightly ajar for 3 hours.

3 Remove meat, and shred with 2 forks. Discard bones, fat and gristle. place shredded meat back into sauce, and cook until li□uid is reduced, 15 to 20 minutes.

4. Apply weed butter as desired

MARIJUANA REUBEN SANDWICH

Ingredients:

2 slices rye bread

1 tablespoon weed butter, softened

2 ounces thinly sliced corned beef

2 ounces sauerkraut

1 slice mozzarella cheese

Preparation:

1. Heat medium skillet over medium heat. Butter bread on one side. Place one slice of bread, buttered side down, in skillet. Layer corned beef, sauerkraut and mozzarella on bread. Top with remaining slice of bread. Cook, turning once, until bread is browned, sandwich is heated through and cheese is melted. Serve immediately.

MARIJUANA LOOSEMEAT SANDWICHES

Ingredients:

2 pounds ground beef

1 teaspoon salt

1/2 teaspoon ground black pepper

1 1/2 cups water

1 onion, chopped

24 slices dill pickle slices

4 ounces prepared mustard

8 hamburger buns

2 tablespoons of weed butter

Preparation:

1. In a large skillet over medium heat, cook the ground beef until brown. Drain. Return to pan with salt, pepper, and water to cover. Reduce heat to low and simmer, uncovered, until water is gone, 15 to 30 minutes.

2. Serve meat on buns topped with chopped onion, dill pickle slices and mustard.

3. Apply weed butter as desired to bun.

MARIJUANA BAKED PIZZA SANDWICH

Ingredients:

1 lb Lean Ground Beef

15 oz Tomato Sauce; 1 Cn,OR 15 oz Pizza Sauce; 1 Cn

1 ts Oregano Leaves

2 c Biscuit Baking Mix

1 ea Egg; Lg

2/3 c weed Milk

8 oz Cheese;

2 oz Mushrooms;Sliced,Drained,1Cn

1/4 c Parmesan Cheese; Grated

Preparation:

Use 1 8-oz package of sliced process American Or mozzarella cheese. Heat the oven to 400 degrees F. Cook and stir the meat in a large skillet until brown. Drain off the excess fat. Stir in half of the tomato sauce and the oregano leaves into the meat mixture. Heat to boiling then reduce the heat and simmer, uncovered, for 10 minutes. While the meat mixture is simmering, mix the baking mix, egg and the weed milk. Measure out 3/4 cup of the batter and set aside. Spread the remaining batter in a greased baking pan 9 X 9 X 2- inches. Pour into the remaining tomato sauce over the batter, spreading evenly. Layer 4 slices of the cheese, the meat mixture, the mushrooms and the remaining cheese on top of the batter and tomato sauce. Spoon the reserved batter on the top of the cheese. Sprinkle the batter top with the grated Parmesan cheese and bake, uncovered, until it is golden brown, 20 to 25 minutes. Cool for 5 minutes before cutting into squares and serving.

MARIJUANA HASH BROWN CASSEROLE

Ingredients:

about 1/2 package of frozen hash browns

4 or 5 eggs

about 1/4 pound of your favorite cheese: shredded, grated, or thinly sliced

(Optional) Grits and salsa and/or Tobasco, etc.

2 Tablespoons of weed butter

Directions:

Add the 2 tablespoons of weed butter into a large skillet. Add hash browns, stirring so the oil coats most of them. Brown the potatoes for about six or eight minutes, stirring occasionally, until the bottom of the pile starts looking golden. As potatoes are browning, beat the eggs and slice or grate the cheese, if necessary. When the potatoes are light golden on the bottom, flip the potato patty over as cleanly as possible, and pour the eggs over the top. Allow this side to brown until the eggs are mostly solidified, around five or eight minutes. Now flip the mixture over again, as cleanly as possible, and then arrange the cheese in a thin layer on top. Cover the pan if possible and allow the cheese to melt (around eight or ten minutes, less if covered). Serve with salsa and grits.

MARIJUANA BAKED TILAPIA

Ingredients

4 (4 ounce) fillets tilapia 2 teaspoons weed butter

1/4 teaspoon Old Bay Seasoning TM, or to taste

1/2 teaspoon garlic salt, or to taste

1 lemon, sliced

1 (16 ounce) package frozen cauliflower with broccoli and red pepper

Directions

Preheat the oven to 375 degrees F (190 degrees F). Grease a 9x13 inch baking dish.

Place the tilapia fillets in the bottom of the baking dish and dot with weed butter. Season with Old Bay seasoning and garlic salt. Top each one with a slice or two of lemon. Arrange the frozen mixed vegetables around the fish, and season lightly with salt and pepper.

Cover the dish and bake for 25 to 30 minutes in the preheated oven, until vegetables are tender and fish flakes easily with a fork.

MARIJUANA FISH TACOS

Ingredients

2 pounds tilapia fillets

2 tablespoons lime juice

2 teaspoons salt

1 teaspoon ground black pepper

1 teaspoon garlic powder

1 teaspoon paprika

cooking spray

2 tablespoons of weed butter

1/2 cup plain fat-free yogurt

2 tablespoons lime juice

1 1/2 tablespoons chopped fresh cilantro

1 1/2 teaspoons canned chipotle peppers in adobo sauce

16 (5 inch) corn tortillas

2 cups shredded cabbage

1 cup shredded Monterey Jack cheese

1 tomato, chopped

1 avocado - peeled, pitted, and sliced

1/2 cup salsa

2 green onions, chopped

Directions

Rub tilapia fillets with 2 tablespoons lime juice and season with salt, black pepper, garlic powder, and paprika. Spray both sides of each fillet with cooking spray. Preheat grill for medium

MARIJUANA MAPLE SALMON

Ingredients

1/4 cup maple syrup

2 tablespoons soy sauce

1 clove garlic, minced

1/4 teaspoon garlic salt

1/8 teaspoon ground black pepper

1 pound salmon

2 tablespoons weed butter

Directions

In a small bowl, mix the maple syrup, soy sauce, garlic, garlic salt, and pepper.

Place salmon in a shallow glass baking dish, and coat with the maple syrup mixture. Cover the dish, and marinate salmon in the refrigerator 30 minutes, turning once.

Preheat oven to 400 degrees F (200 degrees C).

Place the baking dish in the preheated oven, and bake salmon uncovered 20 minutes, or until easily flaked with a fork.

Melt weed butter on salmon once finished cooking.

MARIJUANA GRILLED SALMON

Ingredients:

1 1/2 pounds salmon fillets

lemon pepper to taste

garlic powder to taste

salt to taste

1/3 cup soy sauce

1/3 cup brown sugar

1/3 cup water

1/4 cup THC oil

Directions:

Season salmon fillets with lemon pepper, garlic powder, and salt.

In a small bowl, stir together soy sauce, brown sugar, water, and vegetable oil until sugar is dissolved. Place fish in a large resealable plastic bag with the soy sauce mixture, seal, and turn to coat. Refrigerate for at least 2 hours.

Preheat grill for medium heat.

Lightly oil grill grate. Place salmon on the preheated grill, and discard marinade. Cook salmon for 6 to 8 minutes per side, or until the fish flakes easily with a fork.

MARIJUANA GRILLED MACADAMIA-CRUSTED TUNA WITH PAPAYA SALSA

Ingredients:

2 cups diced papaya

1/2 red onion, diced

1 red bell pepper, diced

1/4 cup chopped fresh cilantro

2 tablespoons lime juice

1 clove garlic, minced

1/4 teaspoon hot chile paste, or to taste

4 (6 ounce) tuna steaks

1/4 cup THC oil

salt and pepper to taste

3 eggs

1/2 cup chopped macadamia nuts

Directions:

Combine the papaya, onion, and red pepper in a bowl. Add the cilantro, lime juice, garlic, and hot chile paste. Toss to combine, then refrigerate until ready to serve.

Preheat an outdoor grill for high heat, and lightly oil grate.

Brush the tuna steaks with olive oil, then season with salt and pepper. Whisk the eggs in a shallow bowl until smooth. Dip the tuna steaks in the egg, and allow excess egg to run off. Press into the macadamia nuts.

Cook the tuna steaks on the preheated grill to your desired degree of doneness, about 2 minutes per side for medium. Serve with the papaya salsa.

MARIJUANA BUTTER

Cooking/Storage Equipment Required:

- A grinder

- A stove to heat the marijuana butter.

- A medium sized heavy duty sauce pan/pot with lid.

- A measuring cup.

- A whisk or a large fork to mix the material with the water/butter solution in the pot.

- Cheese cloth to strain the material before cooling.

- A bowl large enough to hold and cool the Cannabis Butter material.

- A heavy duty plastic wrap to handle and compress the weed butter into a smaller, easier to handle shape.

- A freezable container to store the finished CannaButter.

Ingredients:

- 1lbs of unsalted butter.

- 2cups of water.

- 1 ounce of premium, middle or low grade Cannabis depending on strength preference

Preparation:

Firstly lets grind the Cannabis – Its needs to be nice and fine to make marijuana butter. I'd suggest using a coffee grinder for large amounts. Alternatively hand grinding the Cannabis will definitely help develop your technique!

Cooking:

Bring 2cups of water to a covered boil. Once the water is boiling, add your butter and melt it in the water. Reduce the heat and cover pan so the cannabis butter simmering.

Add the ground Cannabis material to the pan. Once you add the finely ground cannabis powder whisk and mix it into the pot thoroughly. Make sure the solution is nice and smooth, you don't want any lumps in the pot butter crock pot.

Once added replace the lid and simmer on the lowest heat. It's important when cooking

pot butter that you don't burn the bottom of the pan. This will really effect the taste of the CannaButter.

The CannaButter is now ready to simmer and cook for 22-24 hours. This amount of time is important. It is required to extract the THC from the Cannabis. Once finished take the cannabis butter off the heat.

You are now ready to extract the used Cannabis material from the CannaButter solution. This is a really straightforward step, we're just sieving all the little bits of cannabis from the solution, otherwise the cannabis butter will be full of bits.

Place the cheese cloth over an open bowl and ensure that when the li□uid is poured through the cheese cloth will not go with it. Pour the cannabis butter solution into the large bowl.

In the cheese cloth you'll have all the remaining bits of cannabis s□ueeze and extract as much of the solution from the cheese cloth and material as possible.

Cooling:

Place the bowl with the CannaButter solution into the fridge.

Leave it in the fridge until it has set, normally a few of hours. This will separate the fats from the water. The fat being our beautiful Cannabis Butter.

Removing Your Marijuana Butter and Storing:

Removing the CannaButter is tricky. You basically want to scrape out all of the pot butter that's at the top of the bowl, leaving the water and other stuff at the bottom. Use a spoon or spatula.

Once you've collected all the cannabis butter discard the remaining li□uid. Place the cannabis butter in air tight containers and place in the freezer (keeping the CannaButter fresh and the potency high).

MARIJUANA PANCAKES

Ingredients:

2 cups all-purpose flour

2 ½ tsp baking powder

½ tsp salt

1 egg, beaten lightly

1 ½ cups milk

2 tbsp weed butter, melted

Directions:

1. Sift together first three ingredients (to prevent lumps).

2. In a separate bowl, mix egg and milk, then add it to flour mix, stirring until just smooth.

3. Stir in weed butter.

Note: If you want to mix it up, throw in blueberries, a tiny dice of apple, or bits of banana.

4. Grease a griddle or nonstick pan with cooking spray or a little vegetable oil.

5. Heat pan on medium for about ten minutes.

6. Pour batter to form pancakes of whatever size you like.

7. Cook first side until bubbles form on top, about three minutes; then flip and cook other side until it, too, is brown, about two minutes.

8. Serve immediately with weed butter and syrup or hold briefly in warm oven.

9. Once you have learned how to make marijuana pancakes and have eaten them, tell us about your experience in a comment below!

MARIJUANA OLIVE OIL

Marijuana-infused olive oil is a favorite among such renowned Cannabis chefs as Doctor Diane. Depending on the dosage, this medication can severely incapacitate even the most seasoned of Cannabis users. The following is a slightly adapted version of Doctor Diane's famous olive oil recipe.

Ingredients:

1/4 lbs dry bud or dry trimmings

5 cups water (in the pot)

2 cups high-grade olive oil

Materials:

Pressure cooker or crock pot

Grape press or extra-large coffee press pot

1 Medium-length metal spoon

Latex gloves (not the ones with powder on them)

Clean Container

Clean Tupperware

Fine grape press filter or coffee filter

Directions:

Place the 5 cups of water in the pot and bring to a simmer (not a rolling boil). Add the 2 cups of oil and either ¼ lb of dry bud or trimmings. Do not stir, as the moving water will do this for you. Cover and turn the heat down to medium-low. You don't want to cook the water off because this helps to keep your product from burning, and thus wasting the THC. After 20 minutes turn down the heat all the way to low. After an additional 40 minutes (1 hour total) turn off the heat and remove the pressure cooker (or crock pot) from the heat surface. The remaining matter in the pot should look like wet mashed up lawn clippings with much of the liquid remaining.

Next, scoop the matter in your crock pot or pressure cooker into your grape press or press pot. While you are doing this, ensure that you spread the matter evenly in the press, so as to get maximum pressing ability. Pour any remaining liquid into the press, as this is where the majority of the THC is concentrated. Heat up 2 cups of water and pour it over what is in the grape press or press pot. Use a fine filter and tighten this over your clean container with rubber bands or something similar. Next, begin the press the matter, slowly but steadily. The funnel from the grape press should be running into your clean container. The color running through the funnel (if it's clear) should be dark green and gold with some tan intertwined. Make sure you get all of the oil, as you won't want to waste one drop of this precious medication (you may have to tilt the press to get all of the li uid into your container. S ueeze out the filter over your container (this is where gloves come in especially handy, as you can become extremely high just from touching the mix) to get all of the oil. The oil should appear as an inch or so wide layer on top with more water underneath. Place this container in the freezer to solidify overnight.

When you pull the container out of your freezer the next day, you should have a clean Tupperware (or similar container) nearby. Use a metal spoon to scrape off the solidified yet somewhat doughy (it is similar to Play-Doh) mixture and place it in your container. The mix should be a light green color. Any brown matter you see is water and as much of this as possible should be removed. Once you have successfully collected all of this precious mix it will be ready to medicate with. Store it in the freezer or it will go bad.

Warning: ½ cup of this olive oil is equivalent to 1 ounce of marijuana. Use appropriately for your specific needs. This savory treat is great to spread on toasted bread, use in some of your favorite cooking recipes, and even makes for an extremely effective topical medication.

MARIJUANA MILK

Ingredients:

1/4 gallon whole milk (it should be whole milk to work properly)

2 cups heavy whipping cream

1 oz. high-grade buds or trimmings from harvest - again, they should be the uality sugar leaves

1 tsp. vanilla extract

Directions:

Place the whole milk, whipping cream, vanilla and trimmings/buds in a large pot and heat on low/simmer. It's important that you don't set the heat for anything over low/simmer, because you will get milk that has no potency otherwise. Simmer for 2 hours on low. Next, use a cheesecloth or fine strainer (like a coffee filter) to strain the milk once it's done simmering. This ensures that you don't have any unwanted plant matter in your milk concoction. It's better to pour the milk concoction into ice cube trays and freeze them, if you won't be finishing the milk within 48 hours, but if you and friends will finish it by 48 hours, then you can simply refrigerate and drink as you like. Enjoy!

MARIJUANA CHILI CON CARNE

Ingredients:

5 tbsp. canna butter

30 oz. black beans

30 oz. black-eyed peas

30 oz. kidney beans

2 chopped onions

3 chopped tomatoes

1.5 lbs. beef

1/3 cup red wine

3 tbsp. Worcester sauce

2 tbsp. chili powder

2 tbsp. cumin

2 tbsp. crushed red pepper or 1.5 tsp. powdered cayenne

Directions:

In the largest pot you have, place all the beans and peas on low heat. Once steam begins to form, add the wine, all spices and worcester sauce. After 30 to 45 minutes, add the chopped tomatoes and onions, stirring occasionally. Add the cooked beef after you have done this. 20 - 30 minutes before ready to serve, add the cannabis butter. Finish cooking, serve and enjoy. Warning, may cause heartburn.

MARIJUANA BALSAMIC VINAIGRETTE

Ingredients:

3/4 cup extra-virgin cannabis olive oil

3/4 cup balsamic vinegar

2 finely minced cloves of garlic

2 tsp. dijon-style mustard (optional)

1/2 tsp. oregano

Pinch of salt

Pinch of pepper

Directions:

Now for the really hard part: put all the ingredients in a blender and blend until thoroughly mixed. Store in mason jars in the refrigerator.

MARIJUANA MEAT LOAF

Ingredients:

2 lbs. ground beef (or ground meat of your choice)

1/2 oz. finely ground cannabis

1 finely chopped onion

1 chopped tomato

1 chopped stick celery

1 egg

4 pieces toast (crumbled into bread crumbs)

Directions:

First, preheat the oven to 375 degrees Fahrenheit. Then mix all the ingredients together in a large bowl. Make sure the meat you use has a decent amount of fat in it, as you will need it for the THC to be properly activated by the heat and absorbed by the fat and egg. Place the newly formed meat dough in a meatloaf pan and bake for one hour or until the internal temperature has reached 160.

MARIJUANA SPINACH

Ingredients:

1/3 cup cannabis-infused olive oil

1 bunch spinach

5 cloves garlic, minced

1 tsp sriracha sauce (or chili powder)

2 tbsp oyster sauce

1 tsp black pepper Salt to taste

Directions:

Heat the cannabis-infused olive oil in a large saucepan on low. Add the garlic and cook for two minutes, stirring. Add in the chili sauce, oyster sauce, pepper and salt and stir until mixed. Then add the spinach. Cook on one side for about five minutes and then use a spatula to flip the spinach over. Cook on the other side until the spinach becomes tender. Give one final stir before serving and enjoy! Serves four.

MARIJUANA SAUTÉED SQUASH

Ingredients:

3 or 4 pieces yellow suash

1/3 cup cannabis-infused olive oil

6 cloves garlic, minced

2 tbsp soy sauce

1 tbsp garlic powder

1 tsp chili powder

Salt and pepper to taste

Directions:

Heat the cannabis olive oil in a large saucepan on very low. Slice the s□uash into 1/4 inch slices and mince the garlic. Put the s□uash, garlic, soy sauce, garlic powder, chili powder, salt and pepper into the cannabis olive oil. Do not allow oil to boil. Sautee on low until the s□uash becomes soft, overcooking allows it to soak up more oil. Transfer the s□uash to a bowl and drain the leftover oil into a jar to save in the fridge for the next batch. Makes three servings.

MARIJUANA SPAGHETTI

Ingredients:

1/3 cup cannabis-infused olive oil

1 package spaghetti

1 entire bulb garlic, chopped

2 tbsp vegetable oil

1 tbsp soy sauce Parmesan cheese

Salt and pepper to taste

Directions:

In a large pot bring water to a boil. Cook the pasta to desired tenderness. In the meantime, dice the garlic and sautee it in the vegetable oil and soy sauce over medium heat until tender. Turn the heat to low and add the cannabis olive oil. Heat for about five minutes and then set aside. Toss the noodles into the oil and mix in salt, pepper and parmesan cheese to taste. Serves four.

MARIJUANA PIZZA

Medicated pizza is one of the more common edibles found in many dispensaries. The reason why is clear: not only is it a delicious way to medicate, most pizzas are enough to qualify as a meal for patients. This treat is priced around $20 at most dispensaries.

However, a much more rewarding experience can be making your own medicated pizza.

Makes two pizzas.

Ingredients:

Dough:

3 ½ cups flour

1 oz. yeast

1 tsp yeast

8 fl. oz. water

1 tbsp granulated sugar

2 tbsp melted CannaButter (potency depends on dosage of your butter)

Toppings:

2 cups grated cheese of your choice

1 large can of chopped tomatoes

2 tsp freshly ground oregano

Any other desired toppings

5 tbsp melted CannaButter

Instructions:

First, add the flour, yeast and sugar in a large mixing bowl. Then add water and steadily mix it into dough. Cover the bowl with a towel or cloth and set aside in a somewhat warm area for 30 minutes. Uncover, adding the salt and 2 tbsp of melted CannaButter, and mix into a dough ball. Coat this ball in a layer of flour. On a low temperature, simmer any toppings you want in your 5 tbsp of CannaButter. Next, add the tomatoes and oregano and allow to simmer, stirring occasionally, until it is similar to sauce. Now, roll your dough into two separate but even balls. Flatten these and spread your sauce over the dough, subse□uently adding the cheese and any more toppings you want. Bake in the oven for 13 to 18 minutes at 375 degrees.

MARIJUANA MACARONI AND CHEESE

Now, one of your favorite childhood meals is available in medicated form. Macaroni and trees is an especially savory way for many patients to medicate. To make this one-of-a- kind edible, simply add your own Cannabis-infused butter to any homemade macaroni and cheese recipe or even a boxed macaroni and cheese container. Whenever it calls for butter, obviously just substitute the medicated butter for regular. Once you have the butter made, the whole process takes less than 15 minutes, making it one of the fastest ways to make a medicated meal. Enjoy macaroni and trees whenever you fancy it.

Also, due to the fact that the recipe generally does not call for too much butter, it is a good idea to make your Cannabis-infused butter more potent than you normally would. It just depends on your personal preference.

MARIJUANA MASHED POTATOES

Ingredients:

1/2 to 1 stick cannabis butter, depending on potency

4 large potatoes, peeled

1 bunch garlic

1 cup shredded cheddar cheese

1/2 cup sour cream

salt, pepper to taste

dash of olive oil (to roast garlic)

Directions:

First you will want to prepare the roasted garlic. Cut the top off of the bunch and drizzle about a tbsp of olive oil into the garlic. Wrap in foil and bake in the oven for 40-50 mins. Garlic should be tender and come apart with a fork.

While you wait for the garlic to cook, cut the peeled potatoes into cubes and boil them in salted water until tender. Drain the potatoes and mash in a big mixing bowl. Add the cannabis butter, allowing to melt and mix in thoroughly. Then add the sour cream, cheese, roasted garlic, salt and pepper and mix together. Makes about six servings, serve immediately.

MARIJUANA TOMATO BASIL PASTA

Ingredients:

1 lb pasta, preferably spiral or bowtie

4 roma tomatoes

5 cloves garlic, minced

3/4 cup cannabis-infused olive oil

fresh basil

salt and pepper to taste

Directions:

Cook the pasta according to the directions. While the water boils, prepare the sauce. Remove the seeds from the roma tomatoes and dice. Mince the garlic, and chop the basil into strips. Combine the three together in a medium saucepan, heating on low. Add the cannabis-infused olive oil, salt and pepper and stir in. Remove from heat and combine in a separate bowl with the cooked pasta. Makes four very strong servings.

MARIJUANA CILANTRO & SUN DRIED TOMATO PESTO

For a delicious and unique marijuana recipe, spread this pesto on your favorite bread, crackers or as a substitute for pesto pasta.

Ingredients:

1/3 cup medicated extra-virgin olive oil

1 cup chopped fresh cilantro with or without stems

1/2 cup sun-dried tomatoes

1 clove of minced fresh garlic

1 tbsp. finely chopped green chiles or fresh jalapeño

1 tsp. brown sugar

Salt and pepper as preferred

Directions:

It's not critical, but if time permits, soak the sun-dried tomatoes in the olive oil for at least 2 hours. After they have soaked, blend the cilantro, tomatoes, chile or jalapeño, olive oil, garlic and brown sugar until thoroughly mixed together. Take out, serve and enjoy. You can store it in the refrigerator for up to 2 days.

MARIJUANA FRIED BUTTER BALLS

Ingredients:

2 sticks salted canna butter

1/4 cup cream cheese

1 cup flour

1 medium egg

Pepper and dill to taste

1 cup seasoned bread crumbs (Italian seasoning seems to work best) Peanut oil to deep fry balls in

Directions:

Thoroughly mix canna butter, cream cheese, pepper and dill together in an electric mixer. If you don't have one, ensure that you thoroughly mix it together with a spoon. Next, using either a small spoon or melon spoon, make the mixture into separate 1-inch balls and place on a piece of wax paper on a baking sheet. Place in the freezer and leave there until they are completely frozen. Once they are frozen, coat them in egg, then flour and bread crumbs. Place back in the freezer until frozen. After they are frozen, you can take them out and deep fry in peanut oil for 15 seconds on 350 degrees Fahrenheit. Lastly, before you eat them, drain on a paper towel. Enjoy, but be careful, just one or two of these will fully medicate you, even if your butter is of average potency.

MARIJUANA POTATO AND OLIVE OIL SOUP

Ingredients:

8 oz. medicated olive oil

30 oz. water

2 peeled and diced tomatoes

8 chopped slices of bacon

3 large peeled and chopped potatoes

4 chopped garlic cloves

1 large chopped yellow onion

10 peppercorns

3 bay leaves

Salt to taste

Directions:

Heat all ingredients (except potatoes) in large pot for for 15 minutes on 370 degrees Fahrenheit. After the 15 minutes, lower the heat to around 300 - 325, cover and continue cooking undisturbed for another 30 minutes. After the total of 45 minutes is up, add the chopped and peeled potatoes and continue cooking for another 45 minutes. When it's finished, you'll have some very danky and tasty soup. Hint: remove the bay leaves after you're finished cooking the soup.

MARIJUANA ALFREDO PASTA SAUCE

Ingredients:

1/2 stick (1/4 cup) canna butter

1 cup heavy cream (use medicated milk recipe on cream for an even more potent sauce)

2 cloves garlic (minced)

Oregano to taste

1.5 cup fresh-grated Parmesan or Gruyere cheese

1/4 cup freshly chopped parsley

Directions:

First, melt the canna butter in a saucepan on medium to low heat. Add the heavy cream (hopefully medicated) and simmer on the same temperature for 5 minutes. Add the garlic, cheese and oregano and stir or whisk rapidly, while leaving the temperature on medium to low. 1 minute before you're ready to serve, stir in the parsley and pour over your favorite pasta of a savory and medicated treat.

MARIJUANA CHICKEN POT PIE

Ingredients:

1 pound chicken breast, boneless and skinless and diced into cubes

1 3/4 cup chicken broth/stock

1 cup green peas

1 cup diced carrots

1/2 cup diced celery

2/3 cup 2% milk

1/3 cup cannabutter

1/3 cup diced onion

1/3 cup flour

1/2 tsp. salt

1/4 tsp. crushed black pepper

1/4 tsp. celery seed

2 9-inch unbaked pie crusts

Directions:

First, preheat your oven to 385 degrees Fahrenheit (this is very important, any temperature over this will begin to diminish the cannabinoids). In a pan, combine the chicken pieces, peas, carrots and celery and add 1/3 cup water, cover and boil for 15 minutes over medium-high heat. After that, remove it from the heat and place in a strainer to drain. Now, in the same pan, cook the onions in butter (either cannabutter or regular butter) until they are soft and begin the become clear. Now, stir in the pepper, salt, flour, and celery seed, subsequently stirring in the chicken broth and milk (for added potency use canna milk). Simmer this over medium-low heat until the concoction begins to thicken (about 10 - 15 minutes). Next, place the pieces of diced chicken in the pie crusts in separate pans. Pour the heated mixture that you just made over the chicken and into the pie crust and pan. Cover this mixture with the alternate top crust and seal the edges, while trimming away and discarding excess dough. Use a butter knife to cut a half-dozen slits in the top to allow moisture and steam to escape. Place in the preheated oven of 385 Fahrenheit for 40 - 45 minutes, or until the pie is golden-brown on top. Take out and allow to cool for 10 minutes before saving. Enjoy!

Made in the USA
Coppell, TX
21 February 2020